THE FAMILY GROUP.

See page 33.

JAMES BAIRD;

OR,

THE BASKET-MAKER'S SON.

BY THE AUTHOR OF

"FATHER JOHNSON," "THOUGHTS OF HEAVEN," "PRINCE FAMILY," ETC.

New-York:
PUBLISHED BY CARLTON & PORTER,
SUNDAY-SCHOOL UNION, 200 MULBERRY-STREET.

PREFACE.

THE narrative sketched in this little volume will bring before the youthful reader various instructive lessons. In it he will see the importance and blessed results of early piety. That it may lead many a youth to abandon a course of sin, and early to embrace the religion of the Bible, is the prayer of the author.

R. W. A.

FALL RIVER, MASS.,
September, 1852.

CONTENTS.

CHAPTER I.

A FATAL MISTAKE.

CHAPTER II.

AFFECTING RESULTS.

CHAPTER III.

A GOOD SON.

CHAPTER IV.

A SUNDAY SCHOOL.

CHAPTER V.

TRIUMPHANT EXIT.

CHAPTER VI.

GLORIOUS REVIVAL.

CHAPTER VII.

THE WAY TO DO GOOD.

CHAPTER VIII.

WHAT A SUNDAY SCHOOL CAN DO.

CHAPTER IX.

TEMPERANCE MEETING.

CHAPTER X.

THE RECLAIMED.

CHAPTER XI.

TRIUMPHS OF GRACE.

CHAPTER XII.

CONCLUSION.

Illustrations.

JAMES BAIRD.

CHAPTER I.

A FATAL MISTAKE.

In the town of E—— lived a poor family who obtained their livelihood by making baskets. Mr. Baird, the husband and father, had become intemperate, and this was the cause of their poverty. His parents had been respectable and wealthy; and though there was a large family of children, their fortune being divided among them placed each in very comfortable circumstances. Mr. Baird, soon after his marriage, moved to the town of E——, where he built an elegant and commodious house, pleasantly located on a large farm that he had recently purchased.

Though designed as a farm-house, it was admirably arranged for convenience and comfort, and great taste was displayed throughout all its apartments. It occupied a site peculiarly charming: the scenery around was unusually beautiful and enchanting. In one direction, the landscape spread itself out before the eye in its native loveliness. At another point, the hills appeared clothed with verdure, adorned with here and there a group of forest-trees, which presented to the beholder a scene truly picturesque. The meadow land, as it stretched along a beautiful winding river, in another direction, covered with a luxuriant growth of grass, with here and there a cultivated spot, added much to the beauty of the scene. A more desirable location could not have been selected, either for the purposes of agriculture, for health, or for the beauty of natural scenery. Few spots on earth combined so many natural advantages and charming prospects.

Here Mr. Baird commenced business, under very encouraging circumstances. He was out of debt, and had a good farm—the best, it was said, there was in the town. Indeed, he had everything that heart could wish. A more delightful home than his can hardly be imagined. He was greatly respected by all who knew him, and was looked to as soon to become one of the most active and influential men of the town. Already he had been appointed to fill important offices, the duties of which he discharged with promptness and ability.

Mrs. Baird was connected with one of the first families in the town where she lived. She was well educated, possessed an excellent disposition, and was much admired for her personal beauty. Her society was much sought for, and no one in the circle in which she moved was more admired and beloved. At an early age she became pious, and connected herself with a Christian Church. At the age of twenty she gave her hand in marriage to Mr. Baird. The union was highly approved, and all looked upon it as a most happy one. The parents, old and feeble, rejoiced that their children had done so well, and gave them many blessings. The nuptial festival passed off delightfully, and the guests retired, rejoicing in what they had witnessed. It was a bright and happy day—the visions of future domestic bliss and prosperity animated the hearts of the newly-wedded pair. But what changes take place in this changing world! How little we know of what is before us! Our brightest prospects are often soon followed by our greatest sorrows. How many have experienced the sad truth of the following exclamation of an excellent writer: "What scenes of delight, resembling gay visions of fairy bliss, have all been unexpectedly wrapt in shadow and gloom!"

Mr. Baird, with his amiable companion, moved into the new house as soon as it was finished, and commenced housekeeping. Everything went on pleasantly: the

"Perpetual fountain of domestic sweets"

was there. The hearts of the happy pair sweetly blended together, and they were one in their aims, objects, and desires. Mr. Baird cultivated the soil, and received an abundance for his labor. A good Providence smiled upon his efforts, and in everything he did he was prospered. For several years he was contented and happy. Mrs. Baird attended to all her domestic affairs with skill and promptness, ever laboring to make her home a cheerful and happy one: and such it was; everything smiled in and around the dwelling How delightful is such a home!

"Home!
There 's magic in that little word;
It is a mystic circle which surrounds
Comforts and virtues, never known
Beyond the hallow'd limit."

At length some of Mr. Baird's neighbors persuaded him to commence a new business. Distilling cider-brandy was then considered quite a respectable occupation. Some men that stood high for respectability were engaged in it. The temperance reform had at that period scarcely commenced. Mr. Baird yielded to the persuasions of others, and entered into the business.

A beautiful stream of water ran through a part of his farm, over which, at a certain point, he erected a still-house. Cider was abundant, and could be bought cheap. He purchased a large quantity, and made arrangements for running the distillery summer and winter. A large part of the cider was deposited in a sand-bank, near the distillery, for the winter's use. He looked upon the operation as a money-making affair.

His new employment required all his attention, consequently his farm was neglected; but he thought little of this, since, as he imagined, he was in a way of making more money by another business. He was greatly encouraged for a season, and looked forward to a time when he should become independent, and be able to retire from business. But he was doomed to disappointment; adversity, "like an armed man," came upon him. Nothing that he did seemed to prosper. The large cistern or reservoir which contained the cider in the sand-bank gave way, and its contents were soon lost in the river, a few miles below. His brandy had been sold to merchants and others, several of whom failed to pay him. His business, in a short time, became a source of perplexity and trouble to him. He became deeply involved in debt; creditors called, and he was unable to meet their demands.

He did not like to give up his distillery; his proud heart rebelled against the idea of its being said that he had engaged in an undertaking, and was under the necessity of abandoning it: so he resolved to persevere. His companion had long seen that it was going ill with him, and tried to persuade him to give up the business, but all to no purpose.

Six years after he built his distillery, his property was all gone; his creditors came upon him, and took his last cent. Notice came that, by a certain day, he must leave the elegant house he had built.

His broken-hearted wife—now a mother—was overwhelmed with sorrow; such a day she had never expected to see. All her domestic happiness was gone—her home she must leave. Those who professed to be her friends in prosperity had now forsaken her. It was a sad time, indeed,—the sorrows of her heart were inexpressible!

Her husband had become a drunkard: this was her greatest source of grief. His distilling business had not only ruined him in property, but it had destroyed his reputation and character. His companion had observed for some time that he was less attentive to his family, that his business was neglected, and that he was fond of staying at the distillery late at night. Occasionally, he would come home intoxicated, and abuse his family. She still hoped for the best, and thought that he might see his condition, and turn from his evil course; but, alas, it was otherwise! He had already gone too far: his evil habits had taken a strong hold upon him. He grew worse and worse. Soon he neglected his business altogether. He now associated with drinking characters like himself. He was at home but little; and when at home, his presence was dreaded, for he had lost all his kind feelings, and seemed more like a savage. How changed!—how brutalized!

The poor woman kept her feelings to herself, and bore up under her troubles as well as she could. At times, her grief seemed quite insupportable: she thought of her husband,—of what he once was, and what he had now become by intemperance; she thought of the great change that had taken place in their temporal circumstances, and would at times be quite overcome with emotion. She thought, too, of their little son,—the only child that had lived out of four. What would become of him? She saw that the example of the father was calculated to ruin him; she remembered how many sons had been ruined in this way. A young man of fine talents and of great promise, who had been in her husband's employment for several years, had become intemperate through his father's example and influence. She had seen this young man, in his hopes and prospects, crushed by the monster, intemperance. His noble intellect had been ruined, his morals corrupted, his health destroyed, and, though scarcely *thirty*, he had become a mere wreck of what he once was—a poor, sickly, emaciated being, forsaken by his friends, lost to all self-respect, an outcast of society, and soon, in all probability, to find a drunkard's grave!

Mrs. Baird had felt a deep interest for

this young man. She had watched his downward progress, and, in her unwearied efforts to reclaim him, had seen fully the inveteracy of the habit. To think that her *own* and *only* son was to be brought up under an influence calculated to bring him to such a dreadful end was more than she could endure. She resolved, therefore, to do all in her power to prevent his taking the *first step* in the road to intemperance. She saw that a habit of intemperance was not reached at once,—that it was a gradual work,—that it was the *first glass that led to the mischief.* She therefore took every precaution to guard him against the evil, and instilled into his youthful mind the importance of *tasting not* the intoxicating draught. That her efforts were successful will be seen in the sequel.

How strong is a mother's love! What cannot she do to save her offspring from the destroyer! How impressive are her teachings on the youthful mind!

CHAPTER II.

AFFECTING RESULTS.

It was a lovely morning in June. Brightness and beauty seemed to adorn every object of nature: the sun shone brightly, the air was soft and bland, the earth was covered with "its own carpet of beauty," and the birds were skipping from branch to branch, and singing merrily. "Who could not be happy on such a morning?" exclaims one of our youthful readers. But, while the

"Plants and flowers of a thousand dyes
Waved in the soft wind's gentle sighs,"

there were hearts that were sighing, full of grief and sorrow; the loveliness of the morning had no charms for them.

The sad day had arrived when Mr.

Baird and his family were to leave their large and convenient dwelling. It had been built for their especial comfort and accommodation. The out-buildings were well arranged and convenient. The garden furnished an abundance of vegetables and fruit: the fruit-orchard that stood near by had come to maturity, many of the trees of which had been planted by Mrs. Baird's own hands. The beautiful mansion, with its richly-adorned grounds, together with the large and valuable farm, had passed to the ownership of other hands, and they must now leave them forever! A few articles of furniture was all that the law would allow them to take away. It was indeed a sad morning for Mrs. Baird; her feelings may be better imagined than described.

But where were they to go? Let

us describe the place. At the extreme end of the town, near a ravine, at the "brow of a hill," stood an old cottage, which had been tenantless for several months. It had been built for several years, but poorly finished; and such was its present condition, that it was unsuitable as a tenement for any family. It stood near a large tract of wood-land, several rods from a traveled road, and some distance from any other dwelling. Finding no other tenement, the family were under the necessity of taking possession of this uncomfortable one. What a contrast in their circumstances! But Mr. Baird was so far fallen by intemperance that he cared but little for his family,—he seemed to have lost sight altogether of their domestic comfort and happiness.

Their goods being moved, they commenced housekeeping in the miserable and lonely cottage. What pen or pencil can describe the feelings of the broken-hearted wife? But the most terrible affliction of all was that she still had a drunken husband. He who ought to have been her greatest comfort through life, had become the source of all her misery.

"The common calamities of life," says an elegant and popular writer, "may be endured: poverty, sickness, and even death, may be met; but there is that which, while it brings all these with it, is worse than all these together. When the husband and the father forgets the duties he once delighted to fulfill, and by slow degrees becomes the creature of intemperance, there enters into his house the sorrow that rends the spirit,—that cannot be alleviated,—

that will not be comforted. It is here, above all, where she, who has ventured everything, feels that everything is lost. Woman, silent, suffering, devoted woman, here bends to her direst affliction. The measure of her woe is in truth full whose husband is a drunkard. Who shall protect her when *he* is her insulter,—her oppressor? What shall delight her, when she shrinks from the sight of *his* face, and trembles at the sound of *his* voice? The hearth is indeed dark that *he* has made desolate. There, through the dull midnight hour, her griefs are whispered to herself; there her heart bleeds in secret. There, while the cruel author of her distress is drowned in distant revelry, she holds her solitary vigil, waiting, yet dreading, his return, that will only wring from her, by his unkindness, tears even more scalding than those she sheds over his transgression.

"To fling a deeper gloom across the present, memory turns back, and broods upon the past. Like the recollection to the sun-stricken pilgrim of the cool spring that he drank at in the morning, the joys of other days come over her, as if only to mock her parched and weary spirit. She recalls the ardent lover, whose graces won her from the home of her infancy,—the enraptured father, who bent with such delight over his new-born children,—and she asks if *this* can really be he; this sunken being, who has now nothing for her but the sot's disgusting brutality!

"Can we wonder that, amid the agonizing moments, the tender cords of violated affection should snap asunder? —that the scorned and deserted wife should confess 'there is no killing like that which kills the heart?'—that, though it would have been hard for her to kiss for the last time the cold lips of her dead husband, and lay his body in the dust, it is harder to behold him so debased in life that even his death would be greeted in mercy? Had he died in the light of his goodness, bequeathing to his family the inheritance of an untarnished name, the example of virtues that should blossom from the tomb, though she would have wept bitterly indeed, the tears of grief would not have been also tears of shame. But to behold him fallen away from the station he once adorned, degraded from eminence to ignominy,—at home turning his dwelling to darkness, and its holy endearments to mockery,—abroad, thrust from the companionship of the worthy, a self-branded outlaw,—this is the woe that the wife feels to be more dreadful than death, that she mourns over as worse than widowhood."

This picture of the evils of intemperance is truly a melancholy one, but it is life-like,—it is true. How many can tell the sad story of having seen it, in all its appalling features!

The condition of Mr. Baird's family was most deplorable. The heart sickens as one thinks of the circumstances to which they were reduced by intemperance. How dreadful the evil which produces so much degradation and sorrow! We should turn from it as from the most deadly serpent.

"Necessity," it is said, "is the mother of invention." Having made the best arrangements they could for housekeeping, something must be done for a livelihood. Basket-making was fixed on for this purpose. In this Mrs. Baird could render important service. Her husband, by intemperance, had broken down a naturally robust and vigorous constitution, and was able to perform but very little labor. At times, he would assist their little son in procuring materials, and these were wrought into baskets of various kinds, principally under the direction of Mrs. Baird.* The baskets, with what they received in acts of charity, supplied them comfortably with the necessaries of life; and, but for an intemperate husband and father, they might have lived happily, though their outward circumstances were unpropitious. But intemperance is the bane of all domestic peace and comfort.

* See Frontispiece.

Mr. Baird was naturally kind and affectionate, and his affection was strong for his wife and little son; but when under the influence of strong drink his natural affection was all gone, and he seemed more like a demon than a human being. Often would he return from the grog-shop, late at night, to abuse those he once dearly loved. What can destroy affection like intoxicating drinks? What can so brutalize the man, and fill his heart with hatred and cruelty? What can so effectually dry up the fountain of sympathy and degrade man below the beasts that perish? Indeed, under the influence of this dreadful evil, *man is not himself.* Everything that is kind, lovely, noble, and praiseworthy are gone,—his freedom and self-rule are gone,—

——— "He is a weed
Flung from the rock, on ocean's foam to sail
Where'er the surge may sweep,—the tempest's breath
prevail."

But the story of this unfortunate family will be more fully told in the succeeding chapters.

3

CHAPTER III.

A GOOD SON.

James—for this was the son's name—was ten years old at the time his parents removed into the cottage. He was an affectionate child, and early evinced a mild and amiable disposition. Seldom was he ever known to be angry, and he seemed to be a stranger to a revengeful spirit. His plays and pass-times were characterized by gentleness and kindness. On this account he had endeared himself to all his young associates: his company was much sought after by those who had become acquainted with him. There is something peculiarly attractive in gentleness and the loving smiles that accompany it:—

"The sun may warm the grass to life,
 The dew the drooping flower,
And eyes grow bright, and watch the light
 Of autumn's opening hour;
But words that breathe of tenderness,
 And smiles we know are true,
Are warmer than the summer time,
 And brighter than the dew.

"It is not much the world can give,
 With all its subtile art,
The gold and gems are not the things
 To satisfy the heart;
But, O, if those who cluster round
 The altar and the hearth
Have gentle words and loving smiles,
 How beautiful is earth!"

At one time, he indulged in an angry spirit toward one of his playmates; but for this he became truly sorry, and resolved never to cherish such a spirit again. John W——, with whom he was playing, called him hard names, which he resented: thus he was led to show the spirit of anger. He mentioned the circumstance to his mother, who reproved him for his conduct. He felt the reproof keenly, and asked his mother's forgiveness.

At another time, he came near losing his life; a circumstance that made a deep impression on his mind. He had been sent on an errand to one of the neighbors, and was required to return immediately. Here he met with John S——, one of his schoolmates, who urged him to stop awhile for play. At first James was not disposed to listen to his young friend, and even went so far as to say that he must return immediately. "My mother," said he, "told me to come back as soon as I had done my errand."

"Never mind, James," said John; "your mother will not care if you stay a little while. David T—— will be here in a few minutes, and we will have a fine time at play."

James listened, and reluctantly gave his consent to stay a short time. Soon several of their playmates arrived, and their play commenced. Time passed away pleasantly, and before James was aware the sun had nearly set.

"I must go home," exclaimed James; "the sun is almost down!"

"Don't go just yet," said William P——; "let us play a little longer. Our school, you know, commences next week, and I think we ought to have a little time to play during the vacation."

So they continued their play till the sun was quite down.

As James was leaving for home, "Come," said John S——, "let us get some apples. They are ripe on one tree in our orchard, and father said we might have as many as we wished."

Away they ran for the orchard, and soon they were all on the tree. Unfortunately, James made a misstep, and down he came upon the ground; and his head falling on a stone, he was taken up apparently lifeless. The blood ran freely, and for a time it was thought that he would die. He was immediately taken to the house. A physician was sent for, and every effort was made to save the unfortunate boy.

On coming to himself, he thought of his disobedience, and he was much distressed in mind. His mother, who had arrived by this time, tried to console him with the idea that she had forgiven him; and that she doubted not but God would forgive him, if he was truly penitent for his transgression.

James gradually recovered; but the accident made such a deep impression on his mind, that he never dared to disobey his parents again. He was afterward known as one of the most obedient boys in the town.

James assisted his mother much in obtaining a livelihood. He obtained most of the materials for making baskets, and rendered important service in putting them together. The small ones, with the assistance of his mother, he could make very well. The large ones the father assisted in making. He would often carry the baskets to those who had ordered them, and would frequently sell those that were not ordered. His mother preferred to have James sell the baskets, for he always brought the money to her; but when Mr. Baird sold them he would frequently spend the money for intoxicating liquor.

It was a cold day in December, and Mr. Baird had gone probably to waste the day with his drunken companions, leaving his family destitute of bread. James insisted upon taking some baskets, and trying to sell them. Mrs. Baird feared to have him do so, lest he should perish from the severity of the cold; but James was resolute, and was determined to make an effort. He started, and proceeded about two miles without any success. At length he called on Mr. W——, a merchant, who very readily took the baskets, and gave him flour in exchange, and ordered it sent immediately to the residence of Mr. Baird. James hurried back with a glad heart, scarcely feeling the cold, and rejoiced with his mother in his success.

Mrs. Baird gave thanks to the Lord for the supply of flour, which was quite unexpected; for she could but see the hand of God in the success of her son.

James was remarkably attentive to the wants of his mother; he could not bear to see her in want or suffering from any cause; he could not endure seeing her weep. He would often say, "What is the matter, mother? What shall I do for you?" Scarcely did he receive a present, however trifling, without sharing it with his mother. He loved and honored his father, and was attentive to his necessities, but he abhorred his intemperance.

He was very fond of reading, and would interest his mother in reading some good book to her, when not otherwise employed. Many a long winter evening did he spend in this way.

"Pilgrim's Progress," by John Bunyan, was often read; and James would stop and ask questions respecting the characters there introduced. This gave his mother a fine opportunity of explaining to him many interesting subjects respecting a religious life. The Bible was often read by James with much pleasure. Mrs. Baird considered this the book of books, and she felt deeply anxious that her son should early become interested in it. She would often request him to read some of the interesting and thrilling stories of the Old Testament. The story of Moses,—of David and Goliah,—of the children killed by bears,—of the building of the ark,—and of Joseph, sold by his brethren,—were often referred to, and read with attention. These Bible readings were improved by Mrs. Baird, to the great profit of her son. He soon regarded the Bible as the most important of all books,—a mirror in which he was enabled to behold glorious things. The poet has expressed the idea admirably:

"Hold up thy mirror to the sun,
And thou shalt need an eagle's gaze,
So perfectly the polish'd stone
Gives back the glory of his rays.

"Turn it, and it shall paint as true
The soft green of the vernal earth;
And each small flower of bashful hue,
That closely hides its lowly birth.

"Our mirror is a blessed Book,
Where, out from each illumined page,
We see one glorious Image look,
All eyes to dazzle and engage.

"The Son of God: and that indeed
We see him as he is, we know;
Since in the same bright glass we read
The very life of things below."

CHAPTER IV.

A SUNDAY SCHOOL.

About half a mile from the cottage, in one direction, was a small village, in which the manufacturing of various articles—mostly, however, cotton cloth—was carried on. There was no church near, and most of the people in the village seldom, if ever, went to a religious meeting, or even respected the Sabbath as the Lord's day. Some of them were not far removed from heathenism. The children were growing up in ignorance,—spending their Sabbaths in rambling over the fields, and committing depredations on the neighboring farms.

A few of the good people in the town determined on opening a Sunday school there, and secured an old building, located on the brow of a hill near the village, for that purpose. This building had not been occupied for several years, and was quite out of repair. It was formerly the home of a large family, the father of which had died of intemperance; and the mother, being unable to support the family, had gone to live with a relative, while the children were scattered to different parts of the country. Such is often the fate of the drunkard's family.

But the old building, after suitable repairs and alterations, was made to answer very well for the Sunday school. Mr. C——, a young man well known for his piety and his love to children, consented to superintend the school; and a sufficient number of suitable persons volunteered their services as teachers. All necessary preparations having been made, it was agreed that the school should commence on the following Sabbath, and notice was circulated through the village and vicinity accordingly.

It was a delightful Sabbath morning, in June, when the school was opened. About fifty children assembled—some of them for the first time—to learn the Holy Scriptures. It was truly encouraging to see so many assemble at the opening of the school. Most of them were clean and neatly clad, and showed a deep interest in the exercises. Some of the parents and others came to see what was done. The people in the village were generally pleased with the school; though some opposed it, thinking, probably, it would have a tendency to make the children religious.

Among those who were seen winding their way along the side of the hill to the Sunday school was Mrs. G——, with her little children. Her appearance attracted the attention of the superintendent. She was about thirty-five years of age, neatly clad, but appeared much care-worn. Her easy, graceful manner, and her keen, intellectual eye, evidently showed that she had seen better days. During a brief conversation, it was ascertained that she was a daughter of a wealthy merchant in a distant town: that she had enjoyed superior advantages of education, and had been trained in the circles of fashionable life. She was early married to a young man who had just finished his education, and was about commencing business for himself. Her prospects were the most flattering.

Her husband for several years was prosperous in business; but, by an unfortunate speculation, he lost all his property, and became a bankrupt. About the same time he was taken sick. For about five years he was unable to perform any labor, and at length he died without leaving his family a cent on which to depend for a subsistence. Her friends were now unable to assist her, and she was thrown upon her own resources, to obtain a living for herself and children as she could. For awhile she taught school, an employment in which she delighted; but finding her income too limited for her expenses, she resolved to move into a factory village, where she might get situations for herself and two of her children in the mill; leaving the oldest to take care of the house and her younger sister. She had four children at this time, and thought that she thus might better secure a livelihood for them.

Soon after her removal to the village, her oldest daughter sickened and died. In her last moments she found the Saviour precious, and died in great peace. Soon after, her only son was taken sick, and in about a week he died. This was seemingly more than the poor widow could endure; she felt that her main earthly dependence was gone. It was a sad day indeed,—her grief was well nigh insupportable!

"Now," said she, "I am left with these two little girls,—one eleven and the other nine,—and I must provide for them as well as I can. We live here far away from any religious meeting, and the people seem to have no desire for anything of the kind. The children of the village are growing up in ignorance, and many of them are learning bad habits. I rejoice that some good people have resolved on opening a Sunday school here: in no place is one more needed."

The deep afflictions through which the poor widow had passed had been sanctified to her spiritual good. After the death of her eldest child, she resolved on giving her heart to Christ; and though she had no one to pray for her, or to speak to her distressed spirit words of comfort, yet she was enabled to cast herself on the atonement, and was soon able to "rejoice with joy unspeakable, and full of glory." She became an excellent teacher in the Sunday school, and was instrumental of doing much good.

Among the girls present at the school

was one that appeared dejected and sorrowful. The superintendent learned that her mother had recently died; and that her father was a wicked man, but had finally consented that she should go to the Sunday school. The Bible she held in her hand was given to her by her mother, just before she died: she regarded it as a precious treasure. The superintendent gave her excellent advice, which she most gladly received. We shall have occasion to refer to this little girl again in the following pages.

None seemed more interested in the school than did James Baird. He had attended a Sunday school before his parents moved to the cottage; but living now so far from any school of the kind, he had ceased to be a Sunday-school scholar. Now that a school was so near, he most gladly embraced the opportunity of attending.

A more interesting group of children can hardly be imagined. True, some of them looked as if they knew but little about the comforts of life, and nearly all of them were poor as to this world. This may have been their misfortune, but it was not their fault. A finer set of countenances was not often seen. Most of the children appeared very bright and active, and evinced great aptness to learn.

After making suitable arrangements for the school, such as forming the classes, giving out the lessons, &c., and distributing a few books, the superintendent addressed the children on the importance of studying the Bible, urging them to read and love this blessed book.

The following beautiful hymn of Watts was then sung:—

GREAT GOD, with wonder and with praise
  On all thy works I look;
But still thy wisdom, power, and grace,
  Shine brightest in thy book.

The stars that in their courses roll
  Have much instruction given;
But thy good word informs my soul
  How I may climb to heaven.

The fields provide me food, and show
  The goodness of the Lord;
But fruits of life and glory grow
  In thy most holy word.

Lord, make me understand thy law,
  Show what my faults have been;
And from thy gospel let me draw
  Pardon for all my sins.

Here may I learn how Christ has died,
  To save my soul from hell;
Not all the books on earth beside
  Such heavenly wonders tell.

Then let me love my Bible more,
  And take a fresh delight
By day to read these wonders o'er,
  And meditate by night.

The school was dismissed, and the children were soon seen making their way to the village, apparently much delighted with what they had seen and heard. A few were seen crossing the fields, who lived in the farm-houses and cottages in different directions. The superintendent and teachers left the place with glad hearts. Never will they forget that delightful Sabbath morning.

CHAPTER V.

TRIUMPHANT EXIT OF A YOUNG FRIEND.

James Baird, or the basket-maker's son,—for by that name he was generally known,—as we have already informed the reader, felt a lively interest in this school. He was seldom, if ever, absent, unless detained by sickness; and often when quite unwell he would go, when prudence would have led him to stay at home. If confined to the house by sickness, he would converse much about the Sunday school, and express an earnest desire to be there. At such times he would recite his lesson to his mother, who always made it interesting and profitable. This exercise was generally closed by singing a few lines of some appropriate hymn, in which James, when able, always took a part.

James was seldom too late at the school-room. At one time he arrived during the opening exercises, and remained at the door until they closed. On taking his seat, his teacher observed to him, "Well, James, you were rather late this morning." James hardly knew what to say. He tried to find an excuse for his tardiness; but his teacher, seeing his embarrassment, thought it not best to say anything further on the subject, and proceeded immediately to the lesson. The fact was, he lay in bed too late that morning, an unusual circumstance for him, and one he felt ashamed to confess. Such an occurrence did not take place again during his connection with the school. At an

JAMES GOING TO SABBATH SCHOOL.

early hour he would be seen making his way across the fields to the school-room, and frequently he was the first scholar that arrived.

His lessons were always well learned, and he could recite them with great ease and readiness. In this respect he excelled all in his class, which consisted of five lads besides himself. The time which most boys spend in play James spent in studying his Sunday-school lesson. When he came to difficulties which he could not remove, he would go to his mother, who was always ready to assist, and who never failed to render him the necessary aid.

He would often astonish his teacher by his ready answers to the questions proposed; clearly showing that his knowledge of the Scriptures was far in advance of that of most persons of his age. His Sunday-school books were read with great eagerness: the lives and deaths of good children interested him much. His practice was to read his Sunday-school books to his mother; but this was generally done in the absence of his father, who was not much pleased with such kind of reading, and who thought that James was becoming quite too religious.

About this time a circumstance occurred which greatly affected the mind of James, and which was much blessed to the good of his soul. Frank W——, one of the members of his Sunday-school class, was taken suddenly ill, and, after a distressing sickness of about three weeks, passed into the spirit world. Frank, too, was punctual in his attendance, and took a deep interest in the school. He was early left without a mother,—she had died when he was but three years of age,—and his father being from home most of the time, Frank had associated with bad boys, and had contracted many bad habits. His oldest sister, who kept his father's house after the death of his mother, felt deeply interested for "Franky," as he was called, and often tried to prevent his going with wicked associates. When the Sunday school was formed, he was persuaded to attend, and at length became so much interested in it that it was a source of grief to him if circumstances rendered it necessary for him to be absent a single Sabbath. He and James were regarded as the best scholars in the class, and they had become quite intimate.

On learning that Frank was sick, James hastened to see him; but on arriving at his house, he was informed that he was not allowed to see visitors, that he was dangerously sick, and that much depended on his being kept perfectly quiet. This was a great grief to James, as he was very anxious to see his sick friend.

Frank continued to grow worse, and all hopes were given up of his recovery. He was anxious to see his Sunday-school teacher. Being sent for, he immediately came; and on entering the room, he was recognized by the dying boy, who seemed overjoyed at his presence.

"You seem quite sick, Frank," said the teacher.

"Yes," exclaimed the dying boy; "and the doctor says I cannot get well."

He seemed somewhat excited, though

perfectly possessed of his reason. His mind was much exercised about a preparation for eternity. He continued: "I want to go to heaven. I have been trying to give my heart to the Saviour; and I did feel last night that he accepted me as his child. I feel dark now in my mind,—will you pray for me?"

After giving him a few words of counsel, which seemed necessary under the circumstances, the teacher knelt by his bedside, and earnestly prayed that God would fully prepare the child for a home in heaven. During the prayer, Frank felt that Jesus was precious to him, and he soon became unspeakably happy. He was now willing to die, and glad in prospect of soon being in heaven. While the following lines were sung, he seemed filled with unspeakable joy:—

"On Jordan's stormy banks I stand,
And cast a wishful eye
To Canaan's fair and happy land,
Where my possessions lie.

"O the transporting, rapt'rous scene,
That rises to my sight!
Sweet fields array'd in living green,
And rivers of delight."

The day before he died, he wished to see his Sunday-school class. On being sent for, they all came to see their dying friend, and it was a most interesting and affecting meeting. Frank exhorted them all to repent of their sins, and immediately give their hearts to the Saviour.

None were more deeply affected than was James. He had long felt that religion was important, but, like many others, he concluded to defer seeking it till some future time. He now saw what religion could do in the last hours of life, and he made up his mind that he would seek it. Several of his companions came to the same resolution, but only one of them persevered in "well doing."

Frank continued to recommend religion while he lived, and expired praising the Saviour for what he had done for him. He was buried in a small cemetery near the school-room, and on his little grave the Sunday-school children planted many a flower.

Youthful reader, how important is religion to you! What are earth's pleasures when compared with it? It will bless you while you live, and it will comfort and support you when you die. O, seek it without delay!

"Like snow that falls where water glides,
Earth's pleasures melt away:
They rest on time's resistless tide,
And but a moment stay.

But joys that from religion flow,
  Like stars that gild the night,
And the darkest gloom of woe,
  Shine forth with sweetest light.

" Religion's rays no clouds obscure;
  But o'er the Christian's soul
It sheds a radiance calm and pure,
  Though tempests round him roll;
His heart may break 'neath sorrow's stroke,
  But to its latest thrill,
Like diamonds shining when they 're broke,
  That ray will light it still."

CHAPTER VI.

GLORIOUS REVIVAL.

We have already remarked that James had resolved on becoming a Christian. The solemn warnings of his friend Frank, as described in the last chapter, were the principal means of bringing his mind to a decision on this subject. He had, as already noticed, long felt the importance of religion; but seeing religion exhibited in the last hours of his dying friend, as he had never seen it before, he came to the conclusion that he would no longer neglect a subject which he considered of such vast moment. Having made up his mind to this course deliberately, nothing could move him from his purpose. His Sabbath-school teacher soon ascertained that he was anxious about the salvation of his soul, and gave him excellent instruction. His distress of mind was great. He felt that he was a great sinner, and he prayed earnestly that God would have mercy upon him. The prayer of the publican, "God be merciful to me a sinner," expressed the feelings of his heart. His mind was quite dark; and, at times, he hardly knew what to do. Food did not relish, and sleep had well nigh departed from him: the way of salvation by faith he had not yet learned; but he was determined to persevere in the pursuit of his object, let the consequences be what they might.

One Sabbath morning he arose at an early hour, and with a heavy and sin-sick heart repaired to the grove for prayer. It was a beautiful morning;

the air was sweet and balmy; the earth was clothed in its richest attire, and all nature seemed to speak forth its Maker's praise. The birds sang merrily from the branches of the trees, but nothing arrested the attention of James, —his heart was sad and sorrowful. Under a large tree he knelt, and in the deep anguish of his spirit he sought mercy in the forgiveness of his sins. It was an hour never to be forgotten. He cried earnestly to the Lord for help; he agonized in mighty prayer; he felt that he could not leave the place with such a burden upon his heart. He gave up all: he could indeed say,—

> "Here, Lord, I give myself away,—
> 'T is all that I can do."

He said, "Lord Jesus, save me, or I

perish!" Faith took hold on the atoning merit of Christ, and in a moment his soul was set at liberty. What a change! Who can describe it? The trees, the earth, the sky, all seemed to have changed their appearance; everything now appeared lovely,—everything seemed to offer praise to God. The sun had now just begun to throw its rays upon the distant hill tops, and the birds continued their shrill notes among the branches of the trees. James felt that he was in a new world. He was, for the first time in his life, truly happy,—such joy he had never before experienced. He might have exclaimed, "O Lord, I will praise thee; though thou wast angry with me, thine anger is turned away, and thou comfortest me." The language of the poet sweetly described his experience:—

"My God is reconciled,
His pard'ning voice I hear;
He owns me for his child,
I can no longer fear;
With confidence I now draw nigh,
And Father, Abba, Father, cry."

He returned to the cottage, praising the Lord. His mother rejoiced with him; but his father thought that he had been led away by some strange delusion. But James knew that he was happy, and he knew, too, that he had not been deceived. "Whereas, he was once blind, he now saw." He went to the Sunday school, and told his young friends what the Lord had done for him. Many listened to him, and believed what he said. The superintendent proposed, at the close, to spend a little time in prayer. It was an affecting moment. Many wept freely, and some earnestly inquired what they should do to be saved. Such was the feeling manifested, that another meeting for prayer was appointed for that Sabbath evening. And what a meeting it was! Parents and children were seen together weeping, and crying aloud for mercy. Some, too, who had been bitter enemies to religion, were now on their knees in earnest supplication to God. Fervent prayer was offered by several present, and many a sin-sick soul was made to rejoice in the pardoning love of God. James was very anxious for his schoolmates, many of whom he now saw earnestly seeking the Lord.

This revival continued many weeks. About sixty "passed from death unto life." Most of them were persons residing in the village; a few lived in the surrounding country. Among them were persons of nearly all ages; but a large proportion of them were youths, most of whom belonged to the Sunday school.

We have already referred to a little girl, who came to the school with a sorrowful countenance, holding in her hand a Bible which she had received from a dying mother. Her name was Betsey. Her mother was a good woman, and had given her some religious instruction. Soon after the revival commenced, Betsey gave her heart to the Saviour, and experienced the forgiveness of her sins. She felt deeply interested for her ungodly father: she would converse with him on the subject of religion, and earnestly entreat him to seek the salvation of his soul. His hard heart would at times feel deeply affected; but he would resist the

Spirit's influence, and resolve still to pursue his old course.

One evening, as his little daughter was about to retire for the night, she came to her father, and, with tears in her eyes, affectionately besought him to be "reconciled to God." He could scarcely resist the earnest entreaty. He, however, ordered her to go to bed, as if he did not wish to hear anything further from her on the subject. She could not sleep: she commenced praying for her father, for she now felt that all she could do was to carry his case to the Lord.

The wicked man, in passing to his sleeping apartment, heard the voice of his little daughter in prayer. He listened, and soon he heard her say, "O Lord, save my dear father!" This took a deep hold of his heart, and he resolved on becoming a Christian. He spent the night in prayer. In the morning, while earnestly praying in his barn, the Lord spoke peace to his troubled soul.

Betsey now felt that she could desire no more; she was exceedingly happy. Her father could now rejoice with her; and most of the day was spent in prayer and praise.

James had felt a special interest for Chauncey S——, who was regarded as a very bad boy. He had been induced to attend the Sunday school, but when the revival commenced he violently opposed it. He looked upon the revival as a mere excitement, which would in a short time pass away; and he often remarked, that he thought those who had professed to be converted, would, after a few months, return as usual to their old habits and practices. He even went so far as to trifle with the subject of religion, and in one or two instances he was found disturbing the religious exercises. His heart was hard, and the evil spirit at times well nigh took possession of him. Many prayers were offered in his behalf, and the Holy Spirit strove with him. At length he was brought to see himself a sinner, and he earnestly sought "redemption in Christ's blood, even the forgiveness of sins." He had such a sense of his lost condition that he well nigh sunk into despair. His conviction for sin was deep and pungent; and what gave him great trouble was his opposition to the revival: this almost overwhelmed him in deep anguish of spirit.

"I have opposed the revival," he would exclaim; "I have ridiculed the people of God, and have disturbed their religious meetings; can there be mercy for such a sinner as I am?"

A young lady, who had been "made a new creature" during the revival, was made an instrument of good to his soul. She had passed through similar exercises of mind, though she had not gone so far in transgression: she knew how to administer encouragement to his despairing mind; and truly her words were greatly blessed in his salvation. While she was directing him to look to the Saviour for pardon, assuring him that he would turn none away unblest who came truly penitent, light shone into his dark mind, and he felt some degree of comfort within. His peace increased, and in a short time he became very happy in a Saviour's love.

When James heard of the conversion of his friend Chauncey, for whom he had earnestly prayed, he was overjoyed, and immediately went to see him. Their meeting was truly a joyful one: they rejoiced together, "with joy unspeakable, and full of glory."

A Church was formed in the village; and a house of worship was soon erected, in which the word of life was preached every Sabbath.

Thus has God owned and blessed Sunday schools in promoting the work of revivals. Reader, are you a member of a Sunday school? If so, remember that you are highly favored; God has blessed you above thousands of youth. But let not your distinguished privileges aggravate your ruin: "Seek the Lord while he may be found, and call upon him while he is near." Delay not, for thy soul is in danger! The poet has well said:—

MEETING OF JAMES AND HIS FRIEND.

"'Tis but a short, uncertain space,
Allow'd us here to live;
Death, unperceived, comes on apace,
And may no warning give.

"Nor great, nor small, nor old, nor young,
His fatal dart can fly;
The rich, the poor, the weak, the strong,
Without distinction die.

"Each day, for anything we know,
May prove to be our last;
For death may strike the fatal blow
Ere the next hour be past.

"The present moment let us seize,
For this alone is ours;
Now set ourselves our God to please,
With all our active powers.

"To-day, while it is call'd to-day,
Let us regard his voice;
Since danger must attend delay,
Where God has given advice.

CHAPTER VII.

THE WAY TO DO GOOD.

JAMES continued to walk worthy of the profession he had made. He devoted all his time to some useful employment. The subject of religion was the theme of his conversation: whenever he had an opportunity he would recommend religion to others; but few of the youth, especially, escaped his attention. All believed him sincere and pious; and though some thought him too religious, yet they were generally willing to listen to his pious counsels and exhortations.

There was a neighborhood in another part of the town where but very few religious people lived,—most were disposed to ridicule religion. Intemperance and Sabbath-breaking prevailed to a fearful extent. Most of the children neglected the Sunday school. James and one or two of his companions determined to hold a religious meeting at the school-house in that neighborhood. Notice was given of the meeting, but who were to conduct the services was not generally known. Curiosity led many to attend; among them was a man noted for his abilities, a leading man of the town, but who, unhappily, had become quite skeptical in his views of religion.

The meeting was opened by prayer. James and his companions then related, in a simple and unaffected manner, what the Lord had done for them. The word reached many hearts; all felt that a divine influence was resting upon them,

—no outward opposition was manifested. The skeptic to whom we referred had heard nothing like it before: he was astonished at the boldness of the youthful speakers, and the spirit they manifested fully convinced him of their sincerity. He thought that they must possess something above mere natural gifts in order to speak as they had done. On his way home, a friend asked him how he liked the meeting. "They were undoubtedly sincere," he replied; "but it is nothing but boy's play." An arrow of truth had, however, reached his heart, and it was with much effort that he could suppress his feelings: the Spirit of God had taken hold of him in earnest, and he felt that to resist it would be extremely hazardous.

On reaching home, he went to his

barn, and there, for the first time, he bowed his knee in prayer; and such was his distress of mind that he spent nearly the whole night in earnest supplication for the pardon of his sins. In the morning he read the Scriptures, and prayed in his family. Within a few days he obtained a conscious sense of his acceptance with God. He now boldly declared what great things the Lord had done for him. Multitudes of his neighbors became pious, and the work of God went on in great power for several months; nearly every family in the neighborhood became a praying family. The Sabbath was now respected and observed. Thus did the Lord bless the labors of his young servants in promoting his glorious cause.

James delighted much in visiting the sick, and to such he was often made a great blessing. On learning that any of his young friends were sick, he would immediately hasten to their bedside to recommend to them the sinner's Friend. The only child of Mr. W——, the merchant to whom we have already referred, was taken dangerously ill, and all hopes were given up of her recovery. James had known her for some time, as he had often been at her father's house, and had been befriended by the family. He felt a deep interest in her spiritual welfare, and obtained permission to converse with her on the subject. He soon learned that she was conscious of her near approach to eternity; and also that she was exceedingly troubled in mind, feeling that she was unprepared to die.

"Do you think," said Martha, "that God will forgive my sins?"

"O yes," said James; "he has forgiven my sins, and he is willing to forgive yours."

"What shall I do to obtain forgiveness?" anxiously inquired Martha.

"You must be willing to renounce all your sins, and give the Saviour your heart," answered James. "You must also believe that Jesus Christ will accept you as his child. He died to save you; he is interceding for you in heaven now; and, O, how willing he is to save you!"

On leaving, he urged her to give her heart to the Saviour at once; informing her that he would see her again in the morning. During the night she was enabled to receive Christ as her Saviour, and obtained a clear sense of her acceptance with him. On James entering the room in the morning, she exclaimed,

"O, I am happy! The Lord blessed me last night! O, how happy I feel! I am now ready to die!"

James was much rejoiced on finding his young friend in such a happy state of mind. She continued to suffer much in body for about two days, and then died in great peace. Her happy death made a deep impression on the minds of many who witnessed the scene.

Martha was a lovely child,—the idol of the family. Her parents mourned deeply over her departure, but they felt that she was far better off than she could have been in this world of sorrow. They were led to see the uncertainty of all earthly things, and to feel deeply the importance of preparing to meet their daughter in the better land,—

"Where sickness, sorrow, pain, and death,
Are fear'd and felt no more."

CHAPTER VIII.

WHAT A SUNDAY SCHOOL CAN DO.

About this time James read a very interesting story, showing what a Sunday school had accomplished by its effort to do good. This story had a most happy influence on his own mind: hoping it will have a similar effect on other minds, we give the substance of it as follows :—

A little girl, in one of the largest and pleasantest towns in New-England, once proposed to her pastor that the children of his congregation should form themselves into a Juvenile Tract Society. The minister approved of the plan, and the next Sabbath he invited all the children between certain ages to meet at his study, on the next Saturday afternoon. They did so, and he assisted them to form the society. Their tax was to be twelve and a half cents, annually; and the tracts which they received they were first to read themselves, and then to lend or give to others.

After two or three years, however, the monthly tract distribution having gone into operation, it was thought best to relinquish tracts, and do something else with their money. But let us look in a moment upon a meeting of the society, and listen to their deliberations.

Imagine a room filled with little girls, all animated and happy. The center of the room is occupied by a table, upon which are placed paper, pens, and ink. The hour for opening arrives, and all kneeling, unite with their pastor in a short prayer. After the officers for the year are chosen, the question arises, "What shall be done with our money?"

"I should like to give it to the Missionary Society," says one. Others proposed other objects on which to bestow their contributions; but, after some further consultation, the president of the society addressed them as follows:—

"There are many Sunday schools in the country which are almost entirely destitute of a library: I know of some where a book larger than a tract is scarcely to be found. A friend of mine told me of one where the foundation of a library was laid, a few years ago, by stitching together several little tracts of four or five pages each, and covering them with strong brown paper; and that the people had manifested great eagerness to read them. Now, why would it not be a good plan, if we could find some such school, to send it a donation of a little library?"

This plan seemed to strike all favorably, and committees were chosen to carry it into effect. One was to collect the money; another to select books, which were to be examined by the pastor before they were sent; and the third was to prepare a letter. Every part was accordingly attended to: the money was collected, the books purchased, and the letter written. It was decided that their pastor should take the donation with him on a contemplated journey, and find, by inquiry, a suitable school to receive it.

It may be interesting to the reader

to see a copy of the letter. Here it is:—

"As our pastor anticipates making a journey into the western country, we have availed ourselves of the opportunity to supply some destitute Sunday school with a small library; and we hope that the present, although small, will be both acceptable and useful.

"Previously we had purchased *tracts* and *Testaments* for ourselves, with the money; but, being supplied with both, we have concluded to devote it to this object; and hoping that the school on which our pastor shall bestow this library may receive lasting benefit from the perusal of these books, we close by subscribing ourselves,—THE JUVENILE TRACT SOCIETY OF ——."

The scene of our narrative now

changes. We must leave the rich and populous village, and go, in imagination, to a secluded region, on a distant frontier, surrounded by wild mountains and forests, among which the hardy settlers cultivate their scattered farms.

It was Sabbath afternoon: a large covered wagon, drawn by two horses, drove up to the door of the superintendent's farm-house, to take him and his family to the distant Sunday school. The party were soon seated, and rode first through an open field, and then came upon a rough road, which led them, through tangled woods and wild valleys, to a remote district, where the school was established. They crossed rough log bridges; and in some places deep mire, and in others rocks and stumps, obstructed their way.

At length a school-house was in sight.

Behind it was a range of lofty hills, in some places bare and rugged, in others clothed with vegetation to the top. Directly in front was a narrow, cultivated field, and beyond that a dense native forest. The school-house itself stood on the bank of a ravine, through which a mountain torrent found its way at certain seasons of the year. It was a small house, rough in its external appearance, and still more so within.

Several small groups of men and boys were standing around the house, and some little bustle was produced among them by the arrival of the superintendent and his party. As they entered the building, they found the room well filled with the pupils and teachers of the school, and others who had assembled to witness the exercises. There were thirty or forty scholars collected from the families of the settlers, who were scattered among the hills for many miles around. They, with the teachers, occupied the body of the school-house; while the parents and friends, who made the whole number present sixty or seventy, took the other seats.

Poverty was evidently in the homes of many of the children. Some were barefoot; others had come a long way with nothing but handkerchiefs over their heads. All, however, looked clean, healthy, intelligent, and, what was still better, seemed thirsting for instruction in the way to life. The Sabbath school furnished their only opportunity for receiving it.

The school was opened with prayer, and the scholars began their recitations from the Bible. The room was now still, except the low, murmuring sounds that rose from the little groups that surrounded their several teachers. The person whose office was to distribute books, then stepped up to the desk of the superintendent, and taking from it a bundle of old tracts and tattered books, —their only library,—offered one to each of the visitors.

The worn and soiled collection was afterward carried round to the classes, and each pupil had an opportunity to take one; and from the air of satisfaction and pleasure, and sometimes eagerness, with which it was done, it was evident that access to the library, meager as it was, was a valued privilege.

The superintendent then asked a few questions on the lesson of the preceding Sabbath. They were answered with hesitation and reluctance. It might have been doubted whether this proceeded from ignorance or fear, till a mother, who had listened with eager interest to all that had passed, rose and said, earnestly, "Sir, I am sure *our* children remember what you said. They are bashful; they are afraid to speak here, but they have talked about it at home several times."

After an hour spent as usual in the exercises of the school, the signal was given for preparing to close. The superintendent then rose, and opening a little package of books, which was lying on the desk before him, he made a statement somewat as follows:—

"I have some business to bring before the school, before it is closed. In a town several hundred miles from this place, some children, who had formed themselves into a Tract Society, have contributed a sum of money, which they have expended in purchasing eighteen bound volumes of Sunday-school books, for the purpose of presenting them to some newly-established Sunday school. They were sent by their pastor, who has been journeying in this vicinity, and who is now present; and, after some inquiry, he has concluded to offer them to this school."

The expression of gladness which animated all the countenances present showed how the gift was valued.

The superintendent then said, that, as he had supposed an expression of thanks would be proper, he had prepared a letter, which he would read to the school, to see if it met their approbation. The letter was read, and adopted with an eagerness of manner which showed how sincere was their gratitude. All were anxious to get one of the interesting volumes; but as there were not enough to supply each scholar, the books were distributed in the different families.

At last a hymn was sung, and the school was closed. You might, however, have seen the children, as they were returning to their homes, walking along in little groups, earnestly examining their new treasures. And, probably, during the long evenings of the following winter, many a farmer's fireside was cheered by the influence of these volumes; and it is not too much to hope that some were guided by them to purer joys and a more happy home than earth can afford.

Encouraged by this and other examples, James became more and more interested in doing good to his young friends, and his efforts were blessed to the good of many. Multituaes will long remember his pious labors for their good. He took great satisfaction in distributing tracts, which some pious friends had placed in his hands for that purpose. These, in several instances, were instrumental in arresting the attention of the thoughtless, and directing it to the interests of their souls. Some of the happy results of his labors will be seen in the following chapters.

CHAPTER IX.

TEMPERANCE MEETING.

A TEMPERANCE meeting was held, about this time, at the school-house in the neighborhood where James lived. This was something new, as there had been no meeting of the kind held in that part of the town before. These meetings had been held in different places in this and the adjoining towns, but they had met with great opposition. Most of the people used ardent spirit: they considered it indispensably necessary in the time of "haying" and "harvesting;" and on particular occasions, such as being greatly exposed to heat or cold, its use was considered all important. The people generally made cider, which they used very freely as a beverage. Some families consumed not less than thirty or forty barrels a year, besides one or two barrels of cider-brandy.

Large quantities of grain were raised in that part of the country,—it being a farming community,—and most of it was sent to the distillers, and converted into gin or whisky. This article, too, was used very freely: it was not an uncommon thing for some families to use two barrels of gin in a single year. In a community where such a state of things existed, temperance meetings would find but little favor; in some instances, these meetings had been broken up by the rabble.

James, on learning of the appointment of the meeting, resolved to attend, though he made known his intentions to no one at the time. He had heard much said against these meetings, but he was now determined to ascertain their true character for himself. There were but few present, and mostly young persons. Deacon W—— was present, who, for several years, had been known as an active temperance man, and who had been greatly persecuted for the course he had taken on the subject. The lecturer was Mr. C——, a minister of a neighboring parish, who for several years had lectured occasionally on the subject, and in several instances had come near being mobbed while attempting to dissuade the people from using intoxicating liquors. He spoke on this occasion of the evils of intemperance, which he presented in a true and striking light. He named several instances, for illustration, some of which were known to James, and which deeply affected his mind. The case of Mr. W—— was spoken of, who lived in the nearest house to the one in which James resided. It was a sad story, and greatly affected the audience: the particulars were as follows:—

Mr. W—— was the son of Colonel W——, who for some years had been the most wealthy and influential man in the town. His son had been educated at one of the principal colleges in New-England, and early entered upon the practice of law. He married a lady of high standing and of fortune; and settled in life with fine prospects of success in business, and of great social and domestic enjoyment. Everything went on pleasantly and prosperously for a time. They had settled in a pleasant village in C——, and were surrounded seemingly with every blessing that could contribute to make life pleasant and agreeable. They were blessed with three lovely children, who were dear to the parents' hearts.

Mr. W——, unfortunately, associated with those who indulged in the use of intoxicating drinks, and he soon acquired an appetite for them, though at first he used nothing but wines and the more costly liquors. But the appetite for strong drink was soon formed, and it proved his ruin. He gradually lost his extensive and lucrative practice; debts accumulated that he was unable to meet; his health began to fail, and he was obliged to leave the place, and repair to the town where his father then resided. There he was under the necessity of renting a poor tenement, near that of Mr. Baird. Distressed family! Mrs. W—— wept tears of sorrow,—

she was broken-hearted and disconsolate. At times, her anguish seemed more than she could bear. She found a sympathizing friend in Mrs. Baird, who had passed through similar trials. A dark prospect was before her; but she now learned the importance of trusting in the Saviour of sinners.

Her husband continued to grow worse and worse in dissipation, till at length he was unable to attend to any business, and gave himself up almost wholly to the society of the intemperate. On one cold winter's night, returning from a low groggery, where he often spent his evenings in dissipation, and being intoxicated, he fell by the way-side, and there *froze to death!* Such is often the end of the intemperate on earth.

James was well acquainted with the

fatherless children, the oldest being one of his intimate companions. When the above case was referred to by the speaker, James became deeply affected. It brought to mind many things that he had experienced.

At the close of the lecture, a pledge was presented, in nearly the following language:—

"We, the undersigned, do hereby agree not to use distilled liquors as a beverage, nor to furnish them for the use of others."

The speaker observed that the pledge was a simple one,—one that all could understand;—and he wished all that were willing to live up to it to put down their names.

As there seemed to be great backwardness on the part of the people in giving their names, James broke over

CIRCULATING THE PLEDGE.

his embarrassment, approached the table, and wrote his name on the pledge, and urged his young friends to do the same. Several of them followed,—twenty-five signing the pledge, in all. This the lecturer thought was doing well for the first meeting, and appointed another meeting of the same kind, at the same place, in two weeks from that evening.

As the meeting closed, an old gentleman who was present, and who had been a revolutionary soldier, addressed James as follows:—

"My young friend, do you know what you have done to-night?"

"Yes, sir," replied James, frankly: "I suppose you refer to my signing the pledge."

"But did you know that you signed away your liberty?"

"No, sir," said James; "but may I ask, what liberty?"

"Why, you know, I fought for liberty. I suffered too much to obtain it to sign it away as you have done."

"I was aware that you and others fought for our national independence, and this certainly is a very great blessing; but I was not aware that you fought for liberty to drink rum. For my part, I want no such liberty."

The old gentleman soon found that James understood what he was about, and concluded that he had better dismiss the subject, and make his way home.

There was a rumseller present, who used hard words to James because he had signed the pledge. James tried to show him the dreadful nature of his business, but he would not listen, and turned away in a rage,—he could not hear the truth.

The following dialogue is copied, to illustrate the dreadful character of the rumseller's business:—

A company of individuals united themselves together in a "Mutual Benefit Association." The blacksmith comes, and says, "Gentlemen, I wish to become a member of your association."

"Well, what can you do?" was the inquiry.

"O, I can shoe your horses, iron your carriages, and make all kinds of iron implements."

"Very well; come in, Mr. Blacksmith."

The mason applies for admission into the society.

"And what can you do, Mr. Mason?"

"O, I can build your barns, and houses, and stables, and bridges."

"Very well; come in: we can't do without you."

Along comes the shoemaker, and says, "I wish to become a member of your society."

"Well, and what can you do?"

"I can make and mend your boots and shoes."

"Come in, Mr. Shoemaker; we must have you."

So, in turn, apply all the different trades and professions, till, lastly, an individual comes, and wants to become a member.

"And what are you?"

"I am a rumseller."

"A rumseller! What can you do?"

"I can build jails, and prisons, and poor-houses."

"And is that all?"

"No; I can fill them: I can fill your jails with criminals, your prisons with convicts, and your poor-houses with paupers."

"And what else can you do?"

"I can bring the gray hairs of the aged to the grave with sorrow; I can break the heart of the wife, and blast the prospects of the friends of talent, and fill your land with more than the plagues of Egypt."

"Is that all you can do?"

"Come, come!" cries the rumseller; "is not that enough?"

Surely, it is enough! Dreadful business! How many has it ruined, for time and eternity!

CHAPTER X.

THE RECLAIMED.

JAMES now became deeply interested in the cause of temperance, and resolved to do what he could for its promotion. He persuaded many of his young friends to sign the temperance pledge; and distributed a large quantity of temperance tracts, which he obtained of a friend. He became deeply anxious for his father, and, though far gone by intemperance, he hoped that he might be reclaimed.

As the second temperance meeting, already noticed, drew near, he began to persuade his father to attend. At first his prospect of success was very small, but he persevered till he obtained the promise that he would be present at the meeting. This, to James and his mother, was a matter of rejoicing; still, they could hardly anticipate a favorable result. The evening came, and James, with his father and mother, started for the meeting, and arrived just in time to listen to the preliminary exercises. The Rev. Mr. C——, who was to lecture, prayed earnestly that the blessing of God might attend the services of the evening. He prayed especially for that unfortunate class of persons who had brought themselves to disgrace and ruin by intemperance.

During prayer, Mr. Baird seemed much affected, and tears ran freely from his eyes.

The speaker dwelt, in his lecture, particularly on the influence of intemperance on health, property, and domestic and social happiness. Mr. Baird felt the force of what was said, and concluded that he would become temperate; but would not, for the present, sign the pledge. A neighbor of his was present, who had often befriended Mr. Baird, and who felt deeply interested that he should sign the pledge. Mr. Baird could not refuse his earnest solicitations, and, with much apparent reluctance, consented to write his name under the pledge.

Mrs. Baird and James were full of hope, and the moment they saw what was done they could not refrain from giving expression to the overwhelming emotions of their hearts. Tears of joy ran down their cheeks,—such an event they had never expected to see. James and his mother now *felt* that their prayers were answered, and that they ought to give thanks unto the Lord for what he had done. They went home rejoicing.

Mr. Baird now commenced a new course of life. He forsook his old companions, and no longer visited the rum-seller. He gave up his old business of basket-making, and took an adjoining farm to cultivate. Here he found employment for himself and James: they raised a large quantity of vegetables, for which they found an excellent market a few miles distant. They were greatly prospered. The first season they cleared, above all their expenses, a handsome sum. A happier family could not be found: it is true, they had no splendid mansion, nor riches of which to boast; but they possessed, what was far better, social and domestic happiness. Their home had already become delightful.

James continued to take an active part in the Sunday school. He still took great pleasure in getting his lessons; a work which he seldom failed to perform, though he often sat up late on Saturday nights to do it. The Bible had become to him a deeply interesting book, and was read with great satisfaction. His Sunday-school books were read with eagerness, and seldom was one returned without being read once, if not oftener. One Sabbath he returned with that excellent little book, called "The Dairyman's Daughter." Mrs. Baird had read this work some years before, and had spoken of it highly to her son. James commenced reading it at once, and could hardly lay it down till it was finished. Mr. Baird noticed James's special interest in the book, and made some inquiries respecting it.

James most gladly explained to his father the character of the work, and earnestly recommended him to read it, which he consented to do.

James earnestly prayed that the book might be made a blessing to his father. Mr. Baird had read but a few pages before he became interested in it, and the interest increased as he proceeded. When he came to that part of the work where Mr. Richmond describes the dying scene of the Dairyman's Daughter, he became much affected. He clearly saw how grace could enable a Christian to die; and he began to see more fully the importance of becoming a Christian. The Spirit of the Lord was evidently striving with him, and James saw that he had come to a *crisis*,—that he must then decide the point, whether he would give his heart to God or not.

On the following Sabbath, James invited his father to accompany him to meeting, to hear the Rev. Mr. P——, who was expected to preach that day. The meeting was held in the church, near the village already noticed. Mr. P—— preached from the words, "*Ye must be born again.*" It was a close, pointed, searching discourse, and just adapted to Mr. Baird's case. The word reached his heart, and he began to feel that he was a great sinner. His sins now towered before him like mountains, and he felt as though he should sink under them. He returned home with a heavy heart, and deeply oppressed in spirit. James, knowing somewhat the state of his father's mind, proposed in the evening that a portion of Scripture be read, and that a season be spent in prayer. It devolved on James to lead in the services, though he felt it to be a very great cross to do so. It was truly a solemn time. Mrs. Baird was bathed in tears. James tried to pray, but he found it difficult to give utterance to his desires. Mr. Baird groaned in spirit, and seemed to despair of finding mercy.

The time came for retirement, but sleep had departed. James told his father that there was mercy for him,—that, though he had been a great sinner, he might be saved,—that Jesus died to save sinners, even the chief of sinners,—and that he would turn none away unblessed who came to him with a truly penitent heart. He also repeated to him that beautiful hymn, which has been made a blessing to thousands:—

"Come, humble sinner, in whose breast
A thousand thoughts revolve,

Come, with your guilt and fear oppress'd,
  And make this last resolve :—

"I 'll go to Jesus, though my sin
  Like mountains round me close ;
I know his courts, I 'll enter in,
  Whatever may oppose.

"Prostrate I 'll lie before his throne,
  And there my guilt confess;
I'll tell him, I 'm a wretch undone
  Without his sov'reign grace.

"Perhaps he will admit my plea,
  Perhaps will hear my prayer;
But, if I perish, I will pray,
  And perish only there.

"I can but perish if I go—
  I am resolved to try;
For if I stay away, I know
  I must forever die."

The clock struck twelve, and still Mr. Baird seemed pressed under a load of guilt, as a "cart beneath its sheaves." Another season was spent in prayer. Several passages were repeated, containing encouraging promises: the passage, "Come unto me, all ye that labor, and are heavy laden, and I will give you rest," particularly interested him; he felt that he might be one to whom this passage was addressed.

At length he was enabled to trust in the Saviour with all his heart, and he felt that he was accepted. It was a glorious, a memorable hour,—they all rejoiced together. What a change! Now, parents and son could pray together, and rejoice in prospect of meeting in heaven.

Regular family worship was now commenced. The father and the son, and not unfrequently the mother, took a part in the services. They were delightful scenes—such as resemble heaven. Family worship! Many a youth who reads these lines will call to remembrance the occasions when they bowed around the family altar, and when prayer, as holy incense, ascended to the Father of mercies.

The poet, in the following lines, beautifully represents the feelings of many hearts :—

" We will not say the former days
  Were better than our own—
That softer fell the dews of heaven,
  Or the sun more brightly shone—
That the stars look'd down with a sweeter light
  Through the depths of the azure sky—
Or that wandering zephyrs touch'd the notes
  Of a richer harmony.

" For we know Jehovah's word is pledged
  For the sunshine and the dew;
The flowers may fade, but the breath of spring
  Shall their wasted life renew;
And the anthem of nature's praise is hymn'd
  Through changing years the same,
And to countless ages the stars of night
  Their story shall proclaim.

"But we miss, O! we miss, in the homes of men,
The holy song of praise—
The sweet and solemn strain is hush'd,
And we sigh for the former days.
Is the smile of heavenly love withdrawn?
Is the time of blessing o'er?
Have we no more a God in heaven—
A Father to adore?

"Not silent are our blessed dead,
Though their work on earth is done;
The struggle and the gloom are past,
And the glory has begun.
The beauty of the sinless land
Shines radiant on each brow,
And a song of joy and happiness
Is the song they 're singing now.

"Awake, ye children of them who sleep
In the bed of peaceful rest,
And let your voices blend again
With the anthems of the blest!
We know ye learn'd at your fathers' hearth
The hymn of love and praise;
Let us hear your song with your children now—
The songs of your early days!

"O! so sweet on the breath of the balmy air
  Shall the sound of such music be,
That passing angels may pause to hear,
  And rejoice in the melody!
And soft as evening dews that fall
  When no rude wind is stirr'd,
Shall the peace of heaven on that home descend,
  Where the worship of God is heard."

CHAPTER XI.

TRIUMPHS OF GRACE.

MR. BAIRD soon connected himself with the Church, and became a devoted Christian. His neighbors and friends saw the great change which had been wrought, and "took knowledge of him that he had been with Jesus." But his time on earth was now short: his work was nearly done. He was "as a brand plucked out of the burning." Disease had fastened itself upon him with a strong hand; and it was evident to all that he must soon enter the spirit-land.

James became much affected in view of his father's state of health, but felt that all would be right. He had learned to submit to the dispensations of Providence: he felt nothing of the murmuring spirit in his heart, and could say, "The Lord's will be done."

As Mr. Baird declined in health, James was very attentive to his necessities, and did everything in his power to make him comfortable. One night, after a very severe time of coughing,—his disease was consumption,—he seemed much exhausted, and sunk into a state of insensibility. James became much alarmed, fearing he would die immediately. Shortly, however, he revived; and James proceeded to converse with him respecting the state of his mind. Much to his own satisfaction and comfort, his father said, "I feel that my whole trust is in the Lord; and I am confident that he accepts me as his child. O, the goodness of the Lord to me! Most of my life has been spent in transgression: I was far gone in sin, but he had mercy upon me. O, what comfort I have felt since I gave my heart to him!—no tongue can express it! My days are few on earth,—I shall soon be gone. But, O, the glorious prospects before me! I am going home!"

At one time, his joy was so great that he broke out in ecstasy, and praised the Lord with a loud voice. He continued very peaceful, and, at times, triumphant, till he breathed his last. He departed in the full assurance of hope.

"Christ triumphed for his saints," says John Angel James, "by his own death; and he is continually renewing the victory *in them,* amid all the suffering and decay of their own dissolution." "Thanks be unto God who giveth us the victory, through our Lord Jesus Christ."

Mr. Baird's funeral was attended on the Sabbath by a large concourse of people, who followed his remains to their resting place. An appropriate sermon was preached on the occasion, by the Rev. Mr. P——, from the words, "O death, where is thy sting?" &c. He took occasion to refer to what grace had done for Mr. Baird. He regarded it as one of the most striking instances of the triumph of grace he had ever known. "What," said he, "cannot the Lord do! You have seen the great change that has been wrought in your neighbor and friend; you have seen his consistent and devoted life since his conversion; you have seen how he was supported and sustained in his last sickness; and you have seen how he died." He took occasion to exhort his hearers to seek the same great change; not to put it off till old age or a sick-bed, but to seek it now, in youth, in health.

James and his mother were greatly comforted and sustained under their bereavement, and rejoiced greatly in prospect of soon arriving at that world where sickness and sorrow will never come. Glorious world! Sin has never entered there to blast human hopes, or to cause a painful separation of friends. There health, beauty, friendship, and holy communion, will be the portion of the saints. How truthful the following lines:—

"No sickness there!
No weary wasting of the frame away;
No fearful shrinking from the midnight air;
No dread of summer's bright and fervid ray!

"No hidden grief,
No wild and cheerless vision of despair;
No vain petition for a swift relief;
No tearful eye, no broken heart, are there.

"Care has no home
Within that realm of ceaseless praise and song;
Its tossing billows break and melt in foam,
Far from the mansions of the spirit throng.

"The storm's black wing
Is never spread athwart celestial skies!
Its wailings blend not with the voice of spring,
As some too tender floweret fades and dies.

"No night distills
Its chilling dews upon the tender frame:
No moon is needed there! the light which fills
That land of glory, from its Maker came.

"No parted friends
O'er mournful recollections have to weep;
No bed of death enduring love attends,
To watch the coming of a pulseless sleep!

"No blasted flower
Or wither'd bud celestial gardens know;
No scorching blast or fierce descending shower
Scatters destruction like a ruthless foe!

"No battle word
Startles the sacred hosts with fear and dread!
The song of peace, Creation's morning heard,
Is sung wherever angel minstrels tread!

"Let us depart,
If home like this await the weary soul!
Look up, then, stricken one, thy wounded heart
Shall bleed no more at sorrow's stern control.

"With faith our guide,
White-robed and innocent, to trace the way,
Why fear to plunge in Jordan's rolling tide,
And find the ocean of eternal day?"

James was a great comfort to his mother. He continued, for a season, to reside with her, and did everything in his power to make her happy. At length he became convinced that it was his duty to preach the gospel; but such were his views of the proper qualifications of a minister that he was led to cry out, "Who is sufficient for these things?" He felt the importance of acquiring a suitable education; but his means were limited, and he felt bound to provide for the necessities of his mother. A friend, on learning his feelings and circumstances, applied for assistance for him to an Education Society. The application was successful; and, after making arrangements for a comfortable home for his mother, he went to the seminary at W——, where he staid about two years, and made great proficiency in his studies. Here his labors were blessed in promoting a most glorious revival of religion, in which many of his fellow-students became pious. His consistent and uniform course of life was marked by all. He did much, while in the institution, to advance the morals and religious interests of the students.

CHAPTER XII.

CONCLUSION.

We will close this narrative with a few reflections. Permit me, dear reader, to invite your attention to the importance of religion. What treasure so important—so valuable! O, give it a place in your heart! Precious boon!—more valuable than rubies!

"Religion, better, surer treasure
  Than earth's riches can afford;
Hope, and love, and life, and pleasure
  Cluster round that sacred word.

"Envy, pride, and wild ambition
  From its presence fade and die;
The dark storms of guilty passion
  At its gentle bidding fly.

"Here the stricken soul of anguish
  Ease can find for every throe;
Though the heart in grief may languish,
  Here 's a balm for every woe.

"See the wanderer on life's ocean;
Round him angry waves arise;
Toss'd in wild and sad commotion,
Darkness threat'ning from the skies.

"But the clouds have broke asunder;
The shining sun the storm derides;
Hush'd is now the echoing thunder;
See, his bark in safety rides!

"Thus religion, gently beaming,
Bids the storms of anguish cease;
Guides us, by its hallow'd beaming,
To the port of endless peace.

"Turn thy steps, O restless mortal!
Come, O bid thy wand'rings cease!
'T is religion sweetly calling,
'Come, my ways are paths of peace.'"

Who can properly estimate the blessings of early piety? From how many evils does it save—evils to which the youth are so generally exposed? The paths of our feet are beset at every step, and how many of the promising and the fair are enticed away to sin and ruin! Sad to relate, but it is nevertheless fearfully true, that one falls here and another there, before our eyes, and many a parent, in consequence, goes down with sorrow to the grave. Religion affords the only protection and safety. "They that trust in the Lord shall never be moved." "Godliness is profitable unto all things."

Early piety will give firmness and stability to Christian character. By its aid the principles of virtue are fixed deeply and permanently in the heart.

A life of usefulness, too, is intimately connected with early piety. To do good is life's great work; we should live to do good—live to bless our race. Yes, youthful reader, this is *your* work. The poet has expressed the thought, with much force, in the following lines:—

"Live to do good,—an idle wail
Is useless,—action must prevail,
A living pattern teach;
Invoke example's potent aid,
And that to which you would persuade,
Practice as well as preach.

"Live to do good, and kindness show
To neighbor, stranger, friend, or foe,
Nor think the task is hard;
Heaven will bestow its righteous meed,
And every earth-forgotten deed
Shall bring a rich reward."

A life of usefulness will be abundantly rewarded. Thus it was in the case of James, as seen in the foregoing narrative; and thus it will be with all who imitate his example in doing good. But the glorious rewards of heaven await such a life: "Then shall the King say unto them on his right hand, Come, ye blessed of my Father, inherit the kingdom prepared for you from the foundation of the world: for I was an hungered, and ye gave me meat; I was thirsty, and ye gave me drink; I was a stranger, and ye took me in; naked, and ye clothed me; in prison, and ye came unto me. Then shall the righteous answer him, saying, Lord, when saw we thee an hungered, and fed thee? or thirsty, and gave thee drink? or a stranger, and took thee in? or naked, and clothed thee? or sick, or in prison, and came unto thee? Then the King shall answer and say unto them, Inasmuch as ye have done it unto one of the least of these my brethren, ye have done it unto me." "These shall go away into eternal life."

Our short lives will soon be gone: make the most of them for the good of mankind. Time flies swiftly, and how soon it will bear us all away! A few years, and we shall be no more on earth. Are you prepared for death? Thousands as young as you die: some of your former associates and companions have already gone to the tomb. Their smiling faces you see not,—their cheerful voices you hear not,—they are gone! Some of them loved Jesus, and have gone to heaven. You may soon follow them to the spirit-world. O, hasten to give your hearts to the Saviour! Delay not,—there is danger in every moment's delay! As you close this little volume, enter into a solemn engagement with God that you will no longer defer the salvation of your soul.

THE END.

www.ingramcontent.com/pod-product-compliance
Lightning Source LLC
LaVergne TN
LVHW010743120826
845150LV00009B/1879
* 9 7 8 1 4 2 5 5 1 1 0 5 0 *